The Best of **Paul Weller**

£3.92

Wise Publications

London / New York / Paris / Sydney / Copenhagen / Madrid

Exclusive Distributors:
Music Sales Limited
8/9 Frith Street, London W1V 5TZ, England.
Music Sales Corporation
257 Park Avenue South, New York, NY10010, USA.
Music Sales Pty Limited
120 Rothschild Avenue, Rosebery, NSW 2018, Australia.

Order No. AM931953
ISBN 0-7119-5182-9

Book design by Michael Bell Design.
Compiled by Peter Evans.
Photographs courtesy of Go! Discs.

Your Guarantee of Quality:
As publishers, we strive to produce every book to the
highest commercial standards.
The book has been carefully designed to minimise awkward
page turns and to make playing from it a real pleasure.
Particular care has been given to specifying acid-free,
neutral-sized paper made from pulps which have not been
elemental chlorine bleached.
This pulp is from farmed sustainable forests and was
produced with special regard for the environment.
Throughout, the printing and binding have been planned
to ensure a sturdy, attractive publication which should give
years of enjoyment.
If your copy fails to meet our high standards, please
inform us and we will gladly replace it.

Music Sales' complete catalogue describes thousands
of titles and is available in full colour sections by subject,
direct from Music Sales Limited.
Please state your areas of interest and send a cheque/postal
order for £1.50 for postage to: Music Sales Limited,
Newmarket Road, Bury St. Edmunds, Suffolk IP33 3YB.

Printed in the United Kingdom by
Halstan & Co Limited, Amersham, Buckinghamshire.

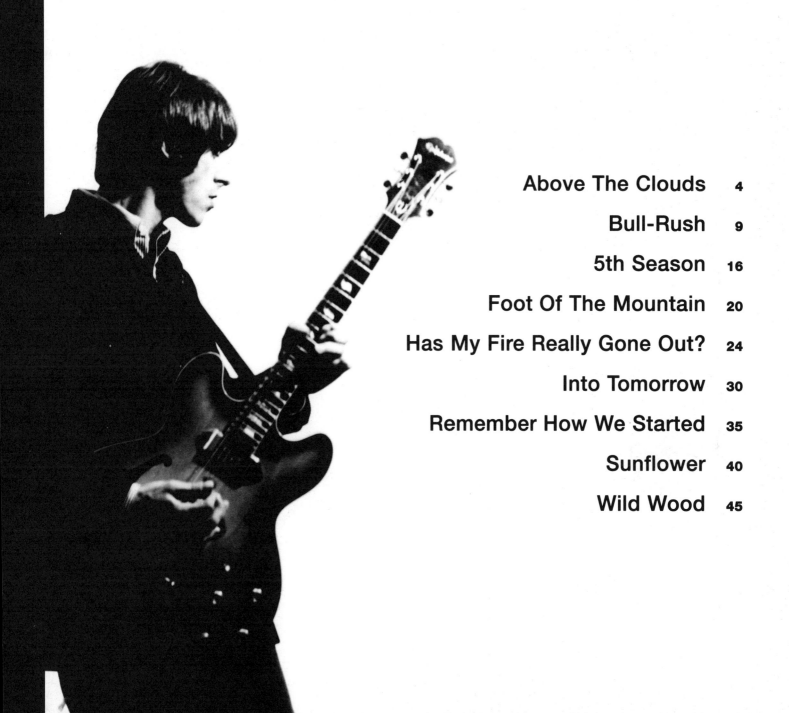

Above The Clouds

Words & Music by Paul Weller

1. Au-tumn blew it's leaves at me, threat-'ning win-ter as I walked.

Sum-mer al-ways goes so quick, bare-ly stop-ping, like my thoughts

so a sad-ness creeps ___ in-to ___ my dreams. When you're scared of liv - ing,

but a-fraid to die, ___ I get scared of giv - ing, and I must find the faith to beat it, oh,

yeh, ___ yeh, yeh.

7

Bull-Rush

Words & Music by Paul Weller

1. In a mo-men-ta-ry lapse of my con-di-tion, sent me tumbl-ing down in-to a deep des-pair,__ lost and dazed so I__ had

no real re-col-lec-tion, un-til the rain___ cleared the air.___

When you wake to find_ that ev - ery-thing_ has left_ you,
2. Like a child too small to reach___ the front door han - dle,

and the clothes you wear_ be - long to some - one else,___
may-be just_ too scared to know___ what I___ would find,_

see your sha - dow chas - ing off to-wards the shore - line,
now I feel_ I'm strong e - nough___ to take the slow_ ride,

I do be-lieve I'm go-ing home,____ 'cause I don't call this place my own,____ I'm miss-ing what I had,____ hap-py times and sad,____ more than I ev-er thought could be.____

5th Season

Words & Music by Paul Weller

1. A storm is rag - ing in - side my
2.3.(see block lyric)

head, — the wind is howl - ing such thoughts of

death. — Why am I so lost — and con-

Verse 2 & 4:
The lightning strikes and the mountains fall,
The sea's come crashing against it all.
Hang on tight in the tides of change
And get your bearings from those still sane.
There's so much I've yet to feel,
Hope the seasons change me too.

Verse 3:
The serpent tangles in the lion's claw,
A cloud of darkness hangs over all.
As fires soar in search of sky,
So blow embers like fireflies.
Hoping love is where they'll lie,
And the season change us too.

Foot Of The Mountain

Words & Music by Paul Weller

Moderately slow

1.3. Like a dream on the o - cean,

al - ways drift - ing a - way, ___ and I ___ can't ___ catch ___

To Coda

— up, she just skips a - way _____ on the tide.

Take me off ___ on your sail-boat ride. ___ Come on now an-gels ___ are

on your side, ___ but she slips ___ a-way ___ oh and nev-er stays.

Verse 2:
Like mercury gliding,
A silver teardrop that falls.
And I will never hold her,
Through my fingers she's gone.
As the foot of the mountain,
Such a long way to climb.
How will I ever get up there,
Though I know I must try.

Has My Fire Really Gone Out?

Words & Music by Paul Weller

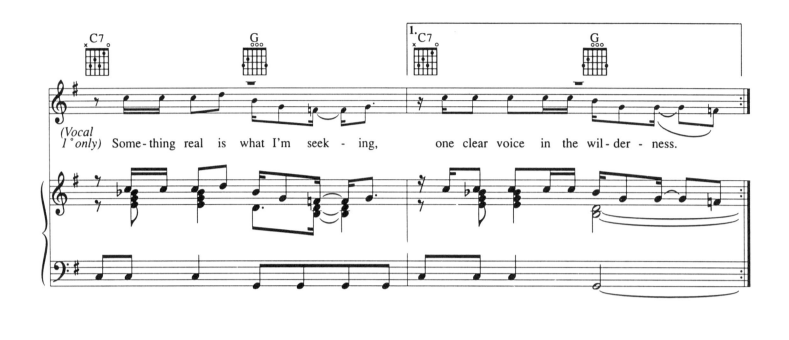

*(Vocal
1° only)* Some-thing real is what I'm seek - ing, one clear voice in the wil-der-ness.

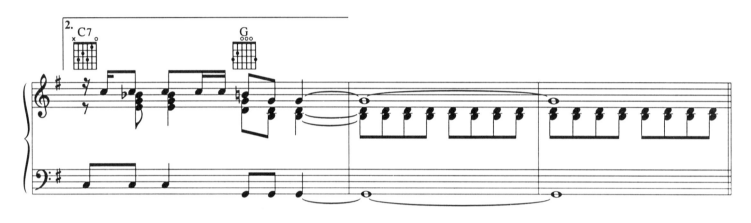

Repeat ad lib.

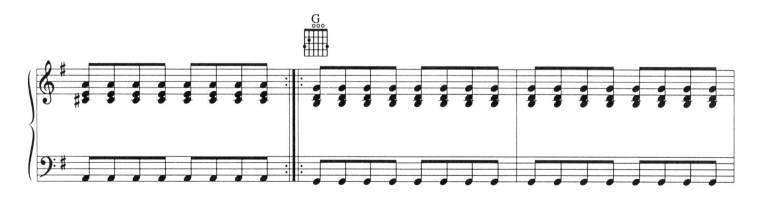

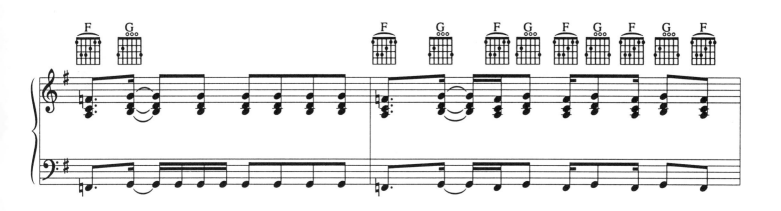

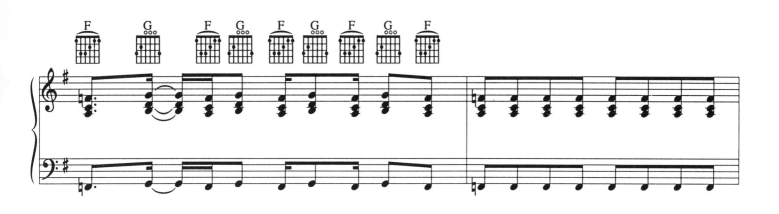

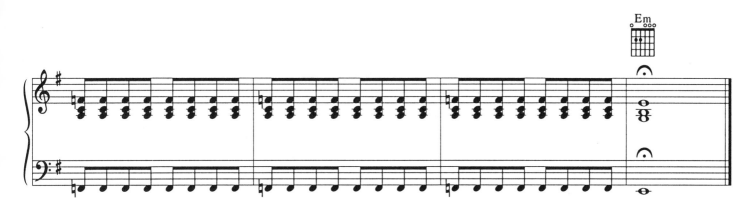

Into Tomorrow

Words & Music by Paul Weller

In-to the mists of time_ and space where we have_ no say_ o-ver date_

_ and place, oh yeh,_ don't get em-bar-rassed if it hap-pens a lot,_ that you

don't know how you start-ed, or where you're gon-na stop,___ oh___ yeh. And

if at times it seems in-sane,___ all the tears and search-ing, turn-ing all___ your joy___ to pain___

in pur-suit___ of learn-ing, buy a dream and hide a - way,___ can't es-cape the sor - row.___ Your

mo-jo will have no___ ef-fect___ as we head in-to to-mor - row.___

Round and round like a twist-ed wheel, spin-ning in__ at-tempt to find__ the feel, the__

__ feel,____ find the path that will help us find a feel-ing of__ con-trol o-ver lives—

__ and minds, ah yeh,__ yeh, yeh, yeh. And if at times it seems in-sane,__

all the tears in search-ing, turn-ing all__ your joy__ to pain in pur-suit__ of learn-ing,

buy a dream and hide a - way,____ can't es - cape____ the sor - row.____ Your

mo - jo will____ have no____ ef - fect____ as we head in - to to - mor - row.____

Yeh, yeh, yeh,____ and

Remember How We Started

Words & Music by Paul Weller

1. Re - mem-ber how we start-ed on a sum-mer's night, too drunk to care a - bout what might? You turned my head to kiss your lips, time stood still as my
2. And if I could I'd take your hand, and lead you off back to the past, I know a trail, a sec - ret mile. Bet - ter to cry than
3. The moon-light shin-ing through your flo - wered cur - tains, I think we knew it was for us cer - tain, and just the thing that we hoped for was build - ing up in - to

Sunflower

Words & Music by Paul Weller

I don't care __
2. *(See block lyrics)*

miss you so,   and I miss you so

now you're gone   I feel so a - lone, ___

oh ___   I miss you so. ___

Verse 2:
Along winding streets we walked hand in hand,
And how I long for that sharp wind to take my breath away again.
I'd run my fingers through your hair,
Hair like a wheatfield, I'd run through.

Verse 3:
I'd send you a flower - a sunflower bright,
While you cloud my days, messing up my nights.
And all the way up to the top of your head,
Sun-shower kisses I felt we had.

Wild Wood

Words & Music by Paul Weller

Verse 2:
Don't let them get you down,
Making you feel guilty about
Golden rain will bring you riches,
All the good things you deserve now.

Verse 3:
Climbing, forever trying,
Find your way out of the wild wild wood.
Now there's no justice,
You've only yourself that you can trust in.

Verse 4:
And I said high tide, mid-afternoon,
People fly by in the traffic's boom.
Knowing just where you're blowing,
Getting to where you should be going.

Verse 5:
Day by day your world fades away,
Waiting to feel all the dreams that say,
Golden rain will bring you riches,
All the good things you deserve now.